Martin Luther King Day

by **Linda Lowery**

illustrated by **Hetty Mitchell**

Carolrhoda Books · Minneapolis, Minnesota

Thanks to the following for permission to reprint quotes in this book: Harper & Row, Publishers, Inc. for quote reprinted on page 21 from *Stride Toward Freedom: The Montgomery Story* by Martin Luther King, Jr. Copyright © 1958 by Martin Luther King, Jr. Reprinted by permission of Harper & Row, Publishers, Inc./Joan Daves for quote reprinted on page 42 from "I Have a Dream" by Martin Luther King, Jr. Copyright © 1963 by Martin Luther King, Jr. Reprinted by permission of Joan Daves./Detroit Free Press, Inc. for quotes by Mrs. Rosa Parks and Mrs. Coretta Scott King reprinted on page 56 from the "Living the Dream" supplement, *Detroit Free Press,* January 14, 1986. Reprinted by permission of the Detroit Free Press, Inc./*Ebony* magazine for quote by Evelyn Ashford reprinted on page 56 from "What Martin Luther King, Jr. Means to Me," January 1986. Reprinted by permission of *Ebony* magazine. Copyright © 1985 Johnson Publishing Company, Inc./*USA Today* for quote by Stevie Wonder reprinted on page 56 from "Amazing Wonder, 'The people's dream has come true'" by Stu Schreiberg, January 20, 1986. Reprinted by permission of *USA Today.*

This book is available in two editions:
Library binding by Carolrhoda Books, Inc.
Soft cover by First Avenue Editions
241 First Avenue North
Minneapolis, Minnesota 55401

Library of Congress Cataloging-in-Publication Data

Lowery, Linda.
    Martin Luther King Day.

    (A Carolrhoda on my own book)
    Summary: Briefly recounts the life of the black minister who devoted his life to civil rights and discusses the national holiday in his name: Martin Luther King Day celebrated on the third Monday of every January.
    1. King, Martin Luther — Anniversaries, etc. — Juvenile literature. 2. King, Martin Luther — Juvenile literature. 3. Afro-Americans — Biography — Juvenile literature. 4. Baptists — United States — Clergy — Biography — Juvenile literature. 5. Afro-Americans — Civil rights — Juvenile literature. [1. King, Martin Luther. 2. Afro-Americans — Biography. 3. Civil rights workers. 4. Clergy] I. Mitchell, Hetty, ill. II. Title. III. Series.
E185.97.K5L65   1987   323.4'092'4[B] [82] 86-20758
    ISBN 0-87614-229-4 (lib. bdg.)
    ISBN 0-87614-468-7 (pbk.)

Manufactured in the United States of America

1 2 3 4 5 6 7 8 9 10 97 96 95 94 93 92 91 90 89 88 87

To children everywhere—
May they have the freedom to dream
and the courage to live their dreams

Author's Note

Martin Luther King, Jr. loved to learn "big words" when he was a boy. As he grew older, he was able to use these words to explain the ideas he believed in. Here are some important words that Dr. King used.

Laws are made to protect our **civil rights**. Those are the rights of all people to enjoy life, freedom, and equal treatment. When a law takes away someone's civil rights and does not protect everyone equally, it is an **unjust law**. When people try to change any unjust condition, they have a choice of taking **peaceful action** or using **violence**. Violence causes hurt to others and damage to property. Dr. King showed people that peaceful action solves problems better than violence does. Talking honestly about problems, marching to make others aware of unjust conditions, and voting for leaders who want to change unjust laws are all peaceful ways to work for change.

We can create change in our own lives by understanding the meaning of these words. Like Dr. King, we can treat others in a just manner and make our homes and our world better by using peaceful action to solve our problems.

It was Monday, January 20, 1986.
Church bells rang out across America.
There were parades in Chicago
and marches in New York City.

Four hundred people rode a "freedom train" across the state of Washington. Why was everybody celebrating?

Leaders from all over the world
met in Atlanta, Georgia.
They talked about peace and justice.

In Arizona, children let
hundreds of balloons fly up
to fill the sky with color.
People were celebrating from Alaska to
Florida, from Hawaii to Washington, D.C.
Why?
It was the first time Americans had
celebrated Martin Luther King's
birthday as a national holiday.
More than 27 countries across
the world celebrated, too.
People talked about how Dr. King had
made the world a better place.
Who was Martin Luther King, Jr.?
How did he make the world better?

Martin Luther King, Jr. was born on
January 15, 1929.
When he was little, his family
called him "M.L."
He lived with his parents, his sister,
and his brother in a big house on
Auburn Avenue in Atlanta, Georgia.

M.L. felt safe and happy in his home.
Three blocks away was another place
M.L. loved to be.
It was the Ebenezer Baptist Church.
His father was the minister there.
His mother led the choir.

M.L.'s parents had some firm
rules for their family.
No matter what the children were doing,
they *always* had to be home for supper.
Suppertime was important.
It was a time for the whole family to
share their ideas and their feelings.
It was at the dinner table that M.L.'s
father and mother taught him one of the
most important lessons of his life.
They taught him to treat all
people with respect.

Not everyone in Atlanta knew how to
treat others with respect.
As M.L. grew older, he saw that
white people and black people
were treated differently.

M.L. and his white friends could not drink from the same water fountains. They could not even use the same public restrooms.

M.L.'s best friend was white.
From the time they could walk,
the two friends had played together
on Auburn Avenue.
Then came their first day of school.
M.L. was sent to a school
for black children.
His friend was sent to a school
with other white children.
After school, M.L. ran
to see his friend.
When he knocked on the door, his
friend's mother said that her son was
too busy to come out and play.
She said he was busy the next
day, too . . . and the next.
M.L. and his friend were never allowed
to play together again.

M.L. finally asked his mother
why he could not play
with his best friend.
M.L.'s mother took him onto her lap.
It was because M.L. was black and his
friend was white, she explained.
His friend's parents didn't want their
son to play with a black child.
M.L. did not understand.
He knew that the color of his skin
should not make any difference
to his friend's parents.
M.L.'s mother held him tight.
"You are as good as anyone,"
she told him.

It just did not seem fair to M.L.
When he grew up, he thought, he
would try to change things.

M.L. worked very hard in school.
He had always loved learning the big
words his father used when he preached.

Now was his chance to learn how
to use those big words.
He hoped that someday he could use
powerful words to tell people
about respecting others.
Martin studied so hard that he
started college when he was only 15.

Martin never stopped thinking about how
he could make the world a better place.
He thought about being a doctor and
helping people when they were sick.
He thought about being a lawyer so
that he could help people who were
in trouble with the law.

Finally Martin made up his mind.
He decided to become a preacher,
like his father and his grandfather.

He went to a school for ministers.
It was there that Martin learned about
Mohandas Gandhi, a man who showed the
people of India peaceful ways to change the
unjust laws of their government.
Gandhi did not use violence.

Martin read everything he
could find about Gandhi.
He began to think about ways he could
use his own preaching to teach others
some of Gandhi's ideas.

Martin went to yet another school, this time in Boston.

By studying even more about being a minister, he earned the title of doctor. Now he was called Dr. King.

While he was living in Boston, he met a woman named Coretta Scott.

They were married on June 18, 1953.

Less than a year later, people from a church in Montgomery, Alabama, asked Dr. King to be their minister.

In Montgomery, black people had been
angry for many years about unjust laws
and unequal treatment.
Dr. King hoped he could help solve
those problems by preaching
about respect and justice.
He and Mrs. King decided
to move to Montgomery.
Soon after they arrived, Dr. King
became more involved in the problems
than he had ever imagined he would.

In Montgomery, black people had to
sit at the back of the bus.
When white people got on
a full bus, black people
had to give them their seats.
It was a law.

On December 1, 1955,
a woman named Rosa Parks got on
a bus after a hard day at work.
She was very tired, and she
was happy to sit down.

The bus driver told Mrs. Parks
to give her seat to a white man.
Mrs. Parks said "No."
She had paid her money to ride the bus.

She wanted to be treated
the same as the white man.
The driver called the police, and they
came and arrested Mrs. Parks.

Many people in Montgomery felt that
Mrs. Parks had not been treated right.
They wanted to change the unjust law.
They asked Dr. King to help them.
Dr. King and other black leaders
worked out a plan.
They asked black people to
stay off the buses so that
the bus company would lose money.

Black people walked or took taxis
or rode together in cars to get to work.

Black people would not ride the buses
until the unjust law was changed.
It took a year and a lot of work
from many people, but finally
Dr. King's plan was successful.
The law was changed.
Black people could sit
in any seat on the bus.
There were other laws in some
southern states that kept white
people and black people separate.
Dr. King wanted to change
those laws, too.
He wanted to change the laws
without violence.
He believed that Americans could make
important changes peacefully.

He went to many cities
to talk to crowds of people.
He said that all people have the right
to equal treatment under the law.
Those rights are called civil rights.

Many people believed in civil rights.
They were willing to work hard to make
sure that everyone had those rights.
Dr. King gave speeches to crowds.
He told the people how to use peaceful
ways to change laws that were not just.

One hot August day in 1963, people
marched in Washington, D.C.
There were people of all colors.
They were old and young, rich and poor.
It was the biggest civil rights
march ever held.
Dr. King stood before the crowd.
"I have a dream today," he said.
"I have a dream that one day...little
black boys and black girls will
be able to join hands with little white
boys and white girls and walk together
as sisters and brothers."
Many Americans also had this dream.
They wanted to help make it come true.

There were some people, though, who did
not agree with Dr. King's words.
They tried to stop him from doing his
work by putting him in jail.
Then he could not talk to crowds.

One winter, someone threw
a bomb at the Kings' house.
Mrs. King ran out with their baby girl.
The explosion just missed them.

At times like this, Dr. King
became sad and discouraged.
He worried about the family he loved.
Sometimes it seemed as if
nobody was listening to his words.
He wondered if he should just stop.
Again and again, he decided
to keep on working for his dream
of equality and justice.

In December 1964, he was given
the Nobel Peace Prize.
It meant that his peaceful work
had been noticed by the world.
Part of the prize was $54,000.
He gave the money to groups of people
who were working for civil rights.

Martin Luther King continued to work
to solve the problems of black people.

Dr. King also worked to help
poor people gain their rights.
He tried to help all Americans
who were being treated unjustly.

In April 1968, he went to Tennessee
to help a group of garbage workers.
While standing on the balcony outside
his motel room, Dr. King was assassinated.
People all over the world were
shocked, angry, and sad.

Though Dr. King is now gone,
he left us with his dream.
Dr. King's work was so important that
many people wanted to honor him.
They wanted to celebrate his birthday
as a national holiday.
The United States as a nation has
honored only one other person
in this way—George Washington.
Fifteen years after Dr. King's death, in
1983, Congress voted to create a holiday
to honor Martin Luther King, Jr.
The first celebration would be in 1986.
President Ronald Reagan signed the bill,
and the holiday became official.
Dr. King's birthday is January 15.
So on the third Monday of every January,
we celebrate Martin Luther King Day.

People fly the American flag.
Children put on plays about the life
of Martin Luther King, Jr.
Children also make signs and paint
pictures that tell what Dr. King's
dream means to them.

People march in parades to show that
they believe in Dr. King's peaceful
ways of solving problems.
Car headlights are turned on at noon.
People march at night with candles.
The lights help people remember how
Dr. King's work lit up the world.
Church bells ring.
The sound reminds people that
Martin Luther King wanted us
to "let freedom ring."

On Martin Luther King Day, we take time to remember what Dr. King did to make our world a better place.

Even more, we try to think of ways that we can live Dr. King's dream each day.

He dreamed of love, peace, and justice.
He dreamed that we can all work together,
no matter what color our skin is.
He worked hard for his dream.
Now it is our turn.

Thoughts on Martin Luther King Day

"I would advise [young Americans] to read, study as much as they can and be concerned enough to think about Dr. King as a man and a leader. As they read and hear, they should...try to find in themselves their own places as citizens in the world."   —Mrs. Rosa Parks, civil rights worker

"One needs to try to follow his teachings. If one follows his teachings, then one surely can live the dream."   —Mrs. Coretta Scott King, president of *The Martin Luther King, Jr. Center for Nonviolent Social Change*

"I, too, believe in the power of dreams. I believe that if we all work hard and attempt to hurdle all obstacles set before us—we can realize our dreams."
—Evelyn Ashford, athlete
and Olympic gold medalist

"Dr. King was blind, too. He didn't see black or white people. He saw only people."
—Stevie Wonder, entertainer